1057 West 14th Street

1057 West 14th Street

Steven Sample

iUniverse, Inc.
New York Lincoln Shanghai

1057 West 14th Street

iUniverse books may be ordered through booksellers or by contacting:

iUniverse
2021 Pine Lake Road, Suite 100
Lincoln, NE 68512
www.iuniverse.com
1-800-Authors (1-800-288-4677)

ISBN-13: 978-0-595-37677-3 (pbk)
ISBN-13: 978-0-595-82060-3 (ebk)
ISBN-10: 0-595-37677-0 (pbk)
ISBN-10: 0-595-82060-3 (ebk)

Printed in the United States of America

Contents

1

In the Beginning

In the beginning, growing up at 1057 West 14th street, I learned a lot. However, first I had to experience a whole lot. I gave respect, trust and learned about responsibility. When I was a little boy about three or four years old I remember seeing my father getting ready to go. I don't remember exactly where, but he was wearing a black pea coat, as they called them back then, with the four buttons on the front and two on the sleeves. It was made out of wool; he also had on a black skull cap. He opened the door, and my mother whom everybody called Rose (short for Rosalie) was carrying me in her arms. She went to the door to tell my father goodbye and she put me down. I looked up and she hugged and kissed my dad and that was the last time I saw my father. I don't recall seeing him after that. I was told my father was shot in the back by a cop and it was a case of mistaken identity.

As time went by my mother had to take care of me and five other kids. The oldest was my brother Terry, then my oldest sister Lesha, my middle sister Neda, my youngest sister Fatty, my next oldest brother Pookey, and last but not least, me, Stevie. Now I know you're wondering what was Rose thinking, naming her children those weird names. All of the names are nicknames that my ma or my grandmother gave us, the Hella tribe, as we were growing up.

My mom had to support all six of us at 1057. She worked as a maid in hotels and in school cafeterias to pay the tuition for our school. Because my mom believe that private schools at the time provided better educational value's and good teachers.,Also worked to put clothes on our backs, shoes on our feet, and food on the table all by herself. Times got hard so she had to put some of us in CPS, which is Chicago Public School. My mom did the best she could with what she had. She's a magnificent mother, provider, and survivor.

Let me tell you a little about my mother and me. She used to take me up north when I was a little boy and take me to the Goodwill or other second-hand thrift stores. She used to take me up there with her all the time, three or four times a week, and I couldn't stand it. She used to buy me blue corduroys with the patches on both knees—my school uniform was blue pants with a white shirt—because she couldn't afford to buy me new uniforms every month; I was rough on clothes, and shoes especially. She also bought me shoes from there as well, which I really hated; those Buster Brown shoes with all the leather worn out around the toes and heel.

I used to hate going to school but I had to go, with my cousins and brothers and sisters and a few other friends. We used to have to walk under a bridge that had a railroad track on top, which had holes and gaps on the bridge, and dogs underneath. To this day I have never seen dogs like the dogs under that bridge. They had patches missing all over their backs their eyes were bloodshot and red, as if they'd stayed up all night waiting for us to come to school the next day. They were wet and smelly, and when we went to school and came home they would chase us back and forth; and my cousin whose name was Butter used to holler and scream, "Run nigga run nigga run!" And I used to tell my mother, but she used to say, "You going to school, and you getting out of here come 7:30 a.m."

My mother used to cook for us and make us fried chicken seven days a week, because they used to have specials on chicken wings. If it wasn't wings it was beans, or when it really got bad, my mama used to say we were on K-rash. That meant no food until check day, whenever that might be in the month. K-rash only lasted less than thirty days, and my brothers and sisters and I used to eat mayonnaise sandwiches and syrup sandwiches and bread balls—that's when you ball up the bread and eat it. I used to cash in bottles that my grandmother saved for me. I could get a dime a bottle and buy penny candy with the money. My mother back then never liked to spend money. She would save any way she could, every penny.

She used to relieve a lot of stress by gardening, tending to the flowers planted in her back and front yard. You need some kind of stress relief raising six kids. My sisters and oldest brother used to tease me and say, "Whatever he wants he gets, whatever that is." They used to tell me and Pookey, my next oldest brother, how spoiled we were, and how we always had our way. Pookey and I always used to fight with each other over stupid stuff like a ride on the big-wheeled bike, or half a can of soda; he was always nitpicking with me.

As I got a little older my Ma met this guy named Cookie; he used to bake and sell cookies and pies. By this time my oldest sister Lesha was pregnant with her first son Inky, and shortly after that my middle sister Neda was pregnant with her first child Mug. Those boys became more like my little brothers to me than nephews. I used to protect them and show them the little things that I knew, even though I couldn't even piss straight yet. I was only about five or six years older. Mug was mostly a good guy, but if you pushed him he would fight you back. Inky was a good guy too but he really wasn't a fighter; he was too cool for that. Mug always fought anybody that messed with his cousin Inky. There was also Jay, who was Fatty's only child and was a good guy too. I looked at him as a blessing because now I felt I had three little brothers instead of nephews, though that's what they were.

Then Rosie was born, Neda's first daughter. She was a little angel. Shortly after that Tony was born. This little guy was (similar to me in ways)because Inky, his brother, used to do some of the same stuff my brother used to do to me. And then there was Annie, Neda's second daughter, who was another angel. Neda's last child was named Lucy, and she was a sweetheart, or should I say still is a sweetheart. As you can see, the Hella tribe has extended to a new generation.

My oldest brother Terry had Popeye, which was his son's nickname, and whom I had fun with every time he was at 1057. Lesha had her last son Rel Rel which is his nick name and was to cool even as a baby. So many events took place at 1057, I should give you a little history on the kids before I get too deep into this story.

My childhood was different compared to some, and it was more unique as I got older and realized what a struggle it was for my mother to put food on the table and clothes on my back. I wanted to work and my sister Neda fixed my birth certificate so that I could work a summer job at the age of twelve. My first job was a summer job in the C.H.A (Chicago Housing Authorities). I loved my job, or should I say, the first check. It showed me a sense of accomplishment, that I could feed and clothe myself. Hasting Street is where I worked in one of the housing projects. I passed out choke sandwiches and cleaned the stairways and swept in front of the buildings.

2

Childhood Experiences

Now let me break down something about those sandwiches, which we called choke sandwiches for a reason. That was because the cheese and baloney on the sandwich was so thick you damn near choked to death trying to swallow it down. Oh, and sweeping outside wasn't as easy as it sounds. We had to wear hard hats at all time because the residents who lived in the building would throw their beer bottles or any bottles that they had out the window of the 10th floor to see if they could hit you in the head—like a video game or something. But despite all that, the job taught me responsibilities, how to depend on myself and help others with the little bit that I had.

As time went on my oldest sister Lesha moved out and left 1057 W. 14th Street and vowed to never move back. I was a little upset because as I said, I looked at my nephews as little brothers, and they were leaving me. But Lesha used to bring them by the house from time to time and I would be happy to see them.

My brother Pookey was a few years older than me, which meant that he would learn how to drive a car and many other things and later teach me. Pookey and my cousin Mike first taught me how to ride a bike. I got my first bike just from old parts that my brother didn't use on his bike, and an old bike that my mom bought me from Jew-town, which is like a big flea market held every Sunday on Halsted and Maxwell Streets.

After getting my bike, and a crash course on how to ride in 60 seconds flat, I was off on my new adventures. I used to get together with a lot of my friends and ride into downtown Chicago. When I saw something in the window of a department store which I liked, I knew of coarse I couldn't afford it, even if I saved all summer to get it. My brothers Terry and Pookey used to make sure my needs were taken care of no matter what, even when I was working at my summer jobs. I remember Terry bought me my first pair of Jordan gym shoes. And Pookey bought me a coat when I didn't have one and needed one to stay warm in the winter. Now to me those are some down a** brothers.

My youngest sister Fatty was a genius. She used to help me with my homework when I used to come home from school. My sister Neda put me up on street games, telling me how not to be so stupid in the streets and to be wise. Now Lesha, she was like a second Mom. She fed me at her house when I didn't have any money or food. I could spend the night there anytime I wanted. She was cool. All of my sisters were cool, so I guess I had some down a** sisters too.

1057 had somethings about it that I will never forget. I remember sitting on my porch and counting cats running by my house; later on I found out that they were sewer rats. Believe it or not, the rats came from this place called the South Water Market, which delivered produce and other food products to major grocery stores.

I look back on those days and reminisce about how I used to ride my bike in the field on the dirt hill and jump on an old mattress and do flips off it. To this day I have a scar on my right elbow from when I flipped off the garbage dumpster and hit my elbow on the corner of the dumpster. Then I ran in the house and blood was everywhere; my mom was in the bathroom and she said calm down, boy. She called a cab and took me to the Cook County hospital to get six stitches.

Anybody from the West Side of Chicago will tell you that anytime you go to the county hospital, it will be an all-day event. That's just the way it was. I don't know why; maybe because a lot of poor people used to go there to get help who couldn't afford high insurance each month.

As I got bigger I used to ride my bike to my grandmother's house. Her nickname was "T." She was a real soldier, or should I say general, because any woman strong enough to raise my mom and brothers and sisiters have to be a veteran in family affairs. I thank God for that lady because without her I would not be here breathing this air today. I used to ride my bike and go to "T's" house and watch cartoons with my cousins Lawrence, Byron, little Fatty, little Willie (Rat), Maurice, etc. There were so many of you, if I fail to mention you, forgive me; you know who you are and I still love you, too. My cousin Lawrence and I used to hang out and watch those classics like Vo-Tron and Spectra-man and Speed Racer and…there are so many I have to ask my cousin what they are; these are just a few I remember.

3

My Partner in Crime

Next door to my grandmother is where I met my first partner in crime. His name was Gilbert, and he and I used to go to elementary school together. We would get in trouble and get sent to the office for making noise in the back of the class, and being class clowns. Some of you may know Gilbert as Nu-Nu from the village which is located in the 'hood. If you saw Nu-Nu you saw me, and vice versa. And if you fought one you had to fight us both. We started getting older and going in different directions, but we remained cool with each other.

There was also this cool guy named Ronald, known as Ron; he and I were real cool at this time. We went to school together as well, and he lived across the street from the school in Circle Park Complex on Roosevelt and Ashland. I started to save my money and bought some Levi's and Nike Airmax, and he and I used to think we were some kind of players with a little game, but you couldn't tell us anything back then. I used to go to the Patio restaurant and pull out a knot of money which really was a twenty-dollar bill, with forty one-dollar bills under the twenty to make it look like I had a lot of money. Not knowing how silly that was, I thought that was cool back then.

At around that same time cousin Lawrence and I were hanging out a little bit. I was getting ready for Dunbar High School and Lawrence was going to Smith Elementary School, and I was telling him about the different high school subjects I was interested in. Lawrence and I had a lot in common that I didn't realize as a kid. I knew about the cartoons and TV shows but I didn't know he liked some of the same music I liked, or favorite movies which we talk about to this day, or cars and so on. I met some of Lawrence's friends who were cool, like Mo and Co Shawn, and Justin, just to name a few.

Getting ready for high school, I started to chill around the neighborhood a little bit more. And that's went I met Nate, who had moved into the "New Home," which was our nickname for the neighborhood. Nate became my new partner in crime; we used to hang out all the time, and Lawrence used to come down to hang out too. Shortly after that, Carl came into the picture; Carl and I used to do some of the same things in the New Home.

I figured we could take over the kids that were our age, because they thought we were crazy or something—which we were, kicking people off bikes on the circle-eight figure in the community playground; wearing masks at night and acting like we were serial killers; all kinds of stuff—if it's silly or crazy we have done it. And Nate and Carl and I were real bad.

Lawrence would just shake his head at us. Lawrence was real cool and relaxed; that's what made him fun to hang around with. Nate was a plum nut and didn't care who knew it; he wasn't ashamed about it. Carl was a daredevil. If you said go do something and you dared him, he would run right out in the middle of the street and do whatever it was you dared him to do. And I was known as the crazy one, who at any time would do all of the above and think nothing of it. So I'm surprised we are all still breathing to this day, with some of the stunts we pulled.

4

Up's and Down's

Life, as we all know, has its ups and downs, and as a young guy I realized you get out of life what you put into it. My Mom told me then (and now to this very day) that people are going to talk about you and try to bring you down no matter what, and they are going to talk about you when things are going good as well. But the bottom line is, people are going to be people. And that's not good or bad, it's just a fact that you have to deal with as long as you breathe here on this earth.

I knew at an early age at 1057 that I wanted to do something with my life. I didn't know what but I knew it was something good. All I knew was that I had big dreams about getting out of the 'hood; and that doesn't mean everything in the 'hood is bad. It's people who make a place the way it is, regardless of whether it's good or bad.

I think back to my mom's friends in the neighborhood, like Ms. Brown, God rest her soul. She was a good lady who made me laugh every time I saw her. She used to sit on her porch and say to me, "What are you going to do today?" and as usual I said nothing. Before the sun set I would get into some sort of trouble, whether it was throwing rocks at truck drivers at the South Water Market or breaking a window or something silly. And she would call my mom and tell her everything, but it took a while to figure that out. I still like Ms. Brown, though, and consider her my buddy.

Growing up was funny like that sometimes. My Mom used to send me to liberty was a mini strip mall that had a grocery store, laundry mat and restaurant from time to time she would send me to get groceries sometimes and I used to get into it with some of the guys in the project buildings. But for some reason that didn't last long, because I used to bring 2x4's, bottles, and bricks to throw at them. Before long they started to call me crazy, but I always used to go by myself because I wanted them to know I didn't need a posse, and if you got me I was definitely going to get you—if not the same day, real soon.

I remember this one incident when these dudes tried to get me in a field, and I ran because there were more of them, but I remembered one of the guy's face and I went to Liberty and was playing the video games and he was washing and I walked outside and found the biggest piece of wood I could find and tried to hit a home run with his head, and asked him if he was so bad now without his posse. People at the laundry mat were saying about me, "The dude is physco." But that ended the running, and later some of those same guys ended up hanging out with me at Newberry Center, and we knew some of the same people. Which was crazy; everybody had their own little groups, yet there was always somebody that knew somebody in a different group?

Meanwhile my brother Pookey moved to my grandmother's house on the West Side. He and I had just established a true brother-like relationship. My cousin Lawrence and I used to ride the L's on the C.T.A. train. And my other cousins Byron and Rat used to already be over there, and we would lift weights and holler at Vince and Pookey and my Uncle about life and see if I could bench press a little bit. I used to get some good advice from them, and use a lot of it to this day.

I used to relax and listen to some Sade, Anita Baker, and Luther in my brother's room, and think about when I would be old enough to leave my ma's house and be on my own like Pookey. Little did I know that it was no rush, and that you should enjoy being a kid and focus on school, that getting a good education should be your number-one goal.

Life at 1057 was good. It had its ups and downs, but I was glad I was raised the way I was by Rosalie Sample—a lady with strength, endurance, and loving care that she shared with all six of her kids. I just wonder sometimes how she did the things she did. When I would come home she made sure to ask how my day was, saying, "Can I warm you up something to eat?" As a kid I didn't realize how much she sacrificed to make sure we had enough even if she didn't. Time after time she instilled in me and my siblings that we can achieve anything we put our minds to. Every time I told her I wanted to do something positive, she supported me, and she still does that to this very day. She is my living inspiration. I have a desire to someday fulfill my hopes and dreams, and I will strive to complete my goals, just because I know how to keep my head up, no matter what. Ma told me that any problem you have will pass in due time, so don't stress, and be the best at what you do.

5

High school Experience's

It's funny like that sometimes, though, learning as a young man how to never give up. When I started high school, walking with people from my 'hood to the bus, I learned my own sense of style from Airmax's, which I wear to this day. I also wore what they called a starter jacket, with a team logo on it; and straight-leg Levi's, and polo shirts, and don't forget the fitted hat to match the jacket. I thought I was clean.

And the girls…it was different then; even in grade school the girls were fully developed and everything. I thought I was a player, trying to have a girlfriend in every class, and I had nine classes as a freshman. No wonder I had to go to summer school the first year.

Some of my partners from the New Home went to Dunbar High School. Lawrence, Gilbert and Li'l Fatty went there for a while and then transferred. I used to know my work and what I had to do in school wasn't hard at all, but I choose to act a fool, when I think about it now. Having my mom come up to the school on that bus in the middle of winter was out of order, just because I was clowning around in class.

As I approached the end of that year I started to get involved in plumbing shop and electrical shop classes, which I liked, learning how to fix stuff that was broken. In those shops they used to have a shop fighting against other shops; for instance the plumbing shop's nickname was Big P, and we used to fight the paint shop and auto body shop.

I was small in the beginning; then I started getting a little bit taller in my second year in Dunbar. So I would grab some of the guys walking past into our shop so my guys could punch them and stuff, just for fun. It was just crazy things like that. When you think about what you wasted your time and energy on, it was just plain nonsense. But as I got a little bit older and a little bit wiser I realized I still had a lot to learn and go through, by trial and error, and that with time it would hopefully get better.

It was funny how life was for me growing up as the youngest of six kids. It was like I always had something to prove. Meaning for instance I had to graduate and get better grades than my siblings; or if they worked at one job while in school, I had to work two jobs—not to be better than them, but just to feel accepted. Because no matter what I did, and even sometimes to this very day, I'm still going to be seen as, "That's my little brother"—which I have grown to accept.

Now getting back to high school, another story comes to mind. Cousin Lawrence, Nate, Carl and I used to ditch summer school. Yeah, I know, it's sad, isn't it, ditching summer school. That's what got me in summer school to began with, not going to class, and hanging out in study hall, and going to the malls, movies, etc. You don't want to know what the "etc." is yet—I'll come back to that later!

Back to ditching summer school, my friend Carl had moved from the New Home and his mom had a two-bedroom apartment on Michigan Ave., which was very nice. Now Carl was the ditch king; it seemed like he didn't ever go to school, so anytime we wanted to cut class or not go at all, we'd call Carl, and he'd be at home just chilling. So one day Lawrence and Nate and I had decided we weren't going to class and were trying to figure out what we were going to do. This is when that etc. stuff kicks in.

We said how about getting some girls from summer school to ditch class and come by Carl's house. Carl's apartment was located around the corner from the high school where we attended summer school There was only one rule: if you were going to bring girls by Carl's house, you had to bring him one too. And let me tell you, this got harder with time, because by the end of the school year those poor girls we took over to Carl's house were traumatized. I say that knowing what I know now, but at the time it was fun just watching some of the things he did to them. From the time we would all walk into the apartment he would jump out from around the corner with a knife or BB-gun and act like he was going to stab them or shoot them, and then after the girl took off running for her life he would say "I'm just playing" and try to talk to them. Most of them ended up liking that nut after they got to know him.

Now my other guy Nate would bring one of his Girls/chicken heads over to the apartment and again traumatize his victims. He would get those girls over there and, Lord have mercy, once that apartment door closed, he would tell the girl to take off her clothes or he would punch her. Now this is the sick part: the girls already knew how he was, so other girls would come over to be treated like this because they heard about what he was doing and they wanted to know if it was true; and yes, it was. He would drag them around the house by their pants leg and they would be hollering and screaming and carrying on. And sometimes this was happening at the same time that Carl was chasing some girl he just met five seconds ago around the house with a knife.

Lawrence was a little bit smoother than that; he would already have a girl ready, if you know what I mean, before we even hit the door. I found out years later that basically he would let them know ahead of time what to expect, giving them some kind of pep talk, and then they would go straight to the back and it was on and popping…without the beatings and traumatizing and so on.

Now I know I had to have some kind of game about myself back then, just to keep one of those cute little girls coming by from time to time with this entire scene taking place. I was somewhat smooth too, because it runs in the family like that, I guess. As a young man my older brother Terry was something to be reckoned with when it came to the ladies. Now watching this dude as I grew up at 1057 W. 14th street, how he treated the ladies, he was smooth like Billy Dee Williams or something. All I would do to those young girls in high school is copy what I saw my older brother do. And before I knew it those fast little girls were doing stuff—well, I can't even tell you what I told them to get them to do it, and it was on and popping. My older brother Terry had so much game back when I was in high school; I saw so many beautiful women come in and out of 1057, it didn't make any sense. I used to just sit on the stairs inside our house and listen to what he was saying and how the women would respond to him. So I knew those girls in school didn't have a chance, because the game I was using wasn't for the average girl. Again, it was funny like that, growing up at 1057; it had its advantages as well as disadvantages. The moral of this part of the story is, know where your children are at all times.

Some of the disadvantages were learning how to balance out my school classes along with my work time and home life. Let me explain to you what I mean. First of all my school grades were average; I could have done more but chose to be a clown at times. My work time became necessary because I liked to dress nice for myself and the girls, and I could talk crazy about what other kids were wearing. As I got older I found out that that was just plain ignorant, because I didn't have a whole lot either. And if I didn't work most of the time, I wouldn't eat; not because my mom didn't cook, but because I got tired of eating chicken everyday. Fried chicken, baked chicken, boiled chicken, grilled chicken, chicken pot pies…and that's just how it was made; I'm not going to mention what parts of the chicken she used. After a while I started looking at the dogs and the cats around the 'hood and wondering what they would taste like fried. And then, I couldn't believed it, but after working in several fast food joints, I started not liking that kind of food as well.

6

Back in the Day

Now as far as home life after school or after work is concerned, it was crazy with my sister's boy friends coming by, and my stepfather and my mom sitting around the kitchen table playing spades/dominoes and drinking Jack Daniels mixed with CocaCola, and smoking cigarettes—my mom smoking Newports and my stepfather smoking Kools. And if you stayed downstairs long enough the special cigarettes would come out.

My uncle Clarence whom we called Dusty, and who was Clarisse's and Butter's father (God rest his soul, he passed away before I completed high school) was something of a weedologist. He was the life of the get-togethers; not just because he was a weed specialist, but because he was always laid back. Even when he cursed you out, it was so smooth and crazy. But he would put those words together like he was a psychologist writing a book on how to beat you're a**. Dusty was a man who fixed his own car and grew his own weed; he didn't think twice about giving you a piece of his mind, but for the most part he was good to me. I used to watch him work on that brown Lincoln Continental for hours and he used to wear these jeans that kind of flare out at the bottom along with a leather jacket with a matching leather hat and leather boots. He had a beard that was always trimmed. Dusty was good to me and even used to throw me a few dollars when my pockets were low.

So back to the late night card games at home while I had school the next day. They would be downstairs yelling and hollering right next to each other. Saying stuff like, "You're set, Jack." "No I'm not, Jim, just play your hand out and see, M.F." Now I remind you there was nobody at the table named Jim or Jack, but in my room and in my mind at three in the

17

morning when I had to be at the bus stop at five-thirty, there were a few M.F.'s—mighty fools, ha ha ha.

The names got worse as the night went on, as they played just to insult one another until somebody got into their true feelings; calling each other names that later became sayings in my everyday life, like "What's up, Jack?" That comes from a drink called Jack Daniels; and there's Jim Beam—to this very day I call my nephews that name and they just laugh; it was funny to me that same way. Ferris, my oldest nephew's father, was one of those who had some good sayings when they were playing at the table. No matter what game they were playing, if he was winning he would look my stepfather right into his bloodshot eyes and say, "You dig buddy," and my stepfather would respond, "Play Jack, we ain't got all night." It was a lot of cursing that I don't want to repeat in this point in my life. These games used to take place at least three times a week, and not just on the weekend, either. So I started spending a few more nights at my Aunt Shirley's house. She's the mother of my cousins Lawrence and Byron, and she also had a pretty little angel named Mary who was a little baby girl at the time, and of course there was Skull, their father. Skull is cool; he is the kind of guy that you wouldn't want to fool with, not with him or his family. He just carried himself that way, but from what I saw by just being around him, I knew he would provide for his family, take care of his family, and teach his kids (as well as me) that life is what you make it, and that it's up to you to get off your backside and do something to accomplish those dreams and goals.

Sometimes I wonder if my father was like that before he died. Even if I didn't have lunch money, or was plain old broke—busted and disgusted—Skull would put a few dollars in my hand at the right time and that would hold me over till I got paid. Lawrence and I would get up in the morning and Lawerence would cut my hair into a box-shaped cut, which was the style back in the late 80s, and I'd get dressed and leave for school. As I was going to the bus stop I would see some of the guys I used too hang with and they would be driving Cadillacs and Acuras and ask if I wanted a ride, and most of the time I used to be like, "No I'm cool" and sometimes I was like, "Let's ride."

But when I used to ride with one of my old partners, he would say, "I see you going to work with that uniform in your bag. And I know you're tried of getting up early in the morning going to school and going back to work right after leaving school. Tell you what–" and he would do this all the time to me—he would pull out a bank roll full of hundreds, and not just a hundred dollar bill and the rest ones. I didn't have to be a rocket scientist to figure out what a seventeen-year-old was doing to make that kind of paper. He would say, "Anyway, let me know when you're tried of making peanuts," and little did I know back then that peanuts would later feed my family. And he would smile and peel off a couple of hundred dollars and say, "Buy yourself something nice, folks."

When you're young and getting money and living in the 'hood where there are people who want what you have and are jealous, you need to watch your back and have a form of security, which eventually this guy got for himself and his family. It's what I call 'hood security—the biggest crazy black guy you can find in the 'hood to watch your back, or sometimes a few of them, depending on your supply of paper (money).

Now as far as haters go, I have been stuck up before, and the first time was the worst time, when I was about seven years old. Now I know you're thinking, who would commit armed robbery on a seven-year-old. Well, I wasn't alone; I was with my mother and my brother Pookey, who at the time couldn't have been any older than ten years old. It took place in the field where you had to cross to get to the stores. We had just left the store called Liberty and my mom had spent her food stamps and bought the usual, some chicken wings and a five-pound bag of potatoes and some canned goods. So we're walking down the field in the middle of the afternoon when this man runs up behind us and points this long black revolver into my mother's back and demands money. My mother turned around and I looked up and I never saw such a look of disgust on her face in my life, even to this day. She said, "You're going to rob me in front of my two boys in the middle of the M.F. field?" She reached in her pocket, pulled out a food stamp book which only had two dollars worth of stamps in it, and said, "Here, take it." And I looked at the hurt in my mother's face and then my brother face, and was in shock as the robber ran across the field dressed in a trench coat with a curl, about six feet tall with dark completion, an African American with Pony's on (a brand of tennis shoe) heading towards the project building.

Life at 1057 W. 14th street had its moments and life-changing experiences which later in life groomed me for some of the best qualities in my life, such as to do what I can to help those who need help, not just financially but spiritually and emotionally, and God bless me, in such a way that hopefully someday somebody reading this book can see that life is not all bad, even if you're going through something bad at this very moment, because you will have a light at the end of the tunnel. And you can share some of your life experiences and help someone.

Pookey and I both believe you have to help those who are willing to help themselves. If not, you will be wasting your time, trying to help someone who doesn't even care about themselves as well as the problem or situation they're dealing with. That's just a little food for thought. Life is truly what you make it, believe or not, and you get what you put into it. It's kind of like the saying, you reap what you sow; I hate to say it but it's true. At this point in my life I don't want to reap anything that's bad anymore, only good things. So it's simple: sow good things and with time you shall reap good things.

Now back to the story. My friend later was locked up for a few years. When he got out he tried to get a job but didn't have much luck, and later began hustling again. Its funny like that in the 'hood; people will front you work or drugs just to get you back in the game, because not only would it make you money, it will make them money as well. Especially if you were known to push a lot of weight in drugs. Someone would be glad to put you on. Getting you back on your feet in no time, with the idea that maybe this time you could do it a little better than the last time.

Today I look at some of the people who are doing this and I shake my head, because not only did I do some crazy stuff myself once, but I see what it does to people up close and personal. I see what it does to a family as well as what it does to a dealer himself. It's addictive in both cases, believe it or not. I used to see the glamour in it, but now all I see is the hurt and pain that comes along with it in the long run.

Some people's situation sometimes dictates what their life choice is going to be, and sometimes it seems to me the drug-dealing, drug-using life is over-rated. What I'm saying is: educate yourself; go to college, get a degree in something you enjoy doing and have a passion for; stay focused; and ask God first and foremost what your vision is, so that you can open up your eyes and have a purpose to why you are here on this earth.

7

Bus Rides

Growing up poor you sometimes had to have an imagination. I used to take the bus on Sunday and ride it into downtown Chicago, and as I looked out the window on Michigan Ave. I would see older men, black and white, driving Mercedes and BMW luxury cars, and their wives with furs and big diamond rings on their hands, and say to myself, what do they do? What is their profession? Do they have a gift, or were they born into a family that's well off? What's it like not having money problems and being able to go to college and not worry about how the tuition's going to get paid?

Of course, like most teenagers, it was time for me to go through my rebellious stage. That's when you tell your mom, "I did not ask to be here and even though we are not rich I still want this and I want that. My friend's parents have a new car, and we take the bus or walk to the store; I hate you!" That's when it happens—Bam Wham Zham! It's like the Batman TV series when she picks up whatever she gets her hands on and busts you upside your head and tells you, "Go live with your friend's parents, then."

And of course back then I wish you would try to call a hot line number. Talking about my mother abusing me—knowing my mom, she would have beat me until they showed up, and gone to jail, and then got out and killed me. That's the problem with society today: there are so many hot lines for kids to call, it's a shame. Ring…"My mother's not feeding me." Ring…"My mother doesn't have hot water." Ring…"My mother doesn't have the lights on." At 1057 West 14th street, all that's just called, welcome to the club.

Now as I'm a little older I realize that a lot of what I was going through would later in life help to build character. When I rode the bus on Sunday I would get what they call a super transfer, so you could ride the bus all day for one paid fare. I sometimes used to not even have enough to get a super transfer, so I would wait till somebody I knew got off the bus on 14th and Haslted in front of Churches Chicken restaurant and ask for their super transfer. I started off going by myself. I knew certain routes by riding on the bus with my mother when I was a little boy. I only used to take my school route on the bus, until I started to venture out on Sundays.

One Sunday I decided to get on the Halsted bus going north, because when I would stay on the bus long enough, I saw that the women's shoes were nice and the men were wearing nice suits and the way the people carried themselves was different.

When I first got on the bus at 14th Street, this is what I'd see on the back of the bus. A man with three cards or three peanuts—let me give you an example of the card hustle and how it works. He would have two black face cards and one red face card and shuffle the cards around and ask you to guess where the red card was. And that was his hustle, until somebody would lose their welfare check and a fight would break out. Because they would be cheating, having somebody working with them winning money and you think there working alone then you play and lose.

Or, you could be riding the bus and there would be pickpockets stealing people's wallets. Or maybe just a thug or hype snatching someone's purse 0r necklace from around their neck. Some of these famous purse snatchers only came out around the first of the month, snatching old ladies' purses after they'd left the check-cashing place having cashed their social security checks.

Those were just a few I have of thousands of stories about the bus. But I would like to take you back to the people I saw up north with the nice homes and nice shoes and nice suits. I never really focused so much on where a person got an item like shoes or clothes; I was more curious about what the person did. I wanted to know, how do I get mine, so I can hold my head up and be proud of how I accomplished it, and so I can show my kids someday that hard work and perseverance and a good attitude pays off in the long run. It wasn't just about getting stuff, because stuff comes and goes. It was more about establishing a sense of pride inside that makes you feel good when you achieve a goal, whether in the long term or short term, and knowing that you and you only can achieve it in a good way. Believe it or not, the moral of this part of the story is that even if you can't afford the latest brand name, you can expose your child to different environments and lifestyles, even if you have to save up to take him or her on a bus ride. In my case it made a world of difference. I knew while growing up that I wasn't the average teenager, because I would watch people and listen to people, especially just to learn. I wanted to learn what to do, what not to do, and how to handle different situations early in life. I learned how to keep my mouth close and to respect my elders.

8

Choice's and Decision's

It wasn't like teenagers nowadays pushing elderly people in front of buses and carrying on. I read in the paper that a nine-year-old boy raped an older lady. Now you tell me what this world is coming to when you've got nine-year-old little boys raping people. It's sad. Where's the parent of this child, and what's the solution to the problem, besides throwing him in a juvenile institution? Nowadays young kids are coming out the womb running the household, and most of the time it's a broken home, meaning both parents are not living under the same roof. Or it's a blended family with a stepparent whom the child doesn't respect from day one. Or maybe, in the new millennium, same-sex families with a child growing up in most cases confused about its own sexuality.

These are days I'm glad my mother beat the hell out of me, so that no way a thought would even enter my mine to do something like that nine-year-old boy did. I drive back around the area where I grew up, and I see some of the same people doing some of the same things I did when I was growing up, and all I can do is pray for them.

I thank God for shining some of his grace and mercy on my life, because without him I know there would be no way I would be where I am today. Moral momentum really does change people; whether it is for the good or for the bad, it changes them. But it's your choice in life as to which roads you travel. Time is truly of the essence; and with the little that you have, cherish it and be glad and know that you are here to make a change. I would hope that in this world we live in, people would help one another in a time of need instead of robbing, killing or destroying one another. It's a known fact that the human being only uses a small portion of his or her brain, and I think it's time for us to turn it up a notch and pay attention to our kids, and if you are a parent, to better yourself as well and get off the system.

Now if you are handicapped, or if you have a special need and truly need help from the system and it works for you, that's OK. But I'm talking about those that are receiving welfare in six different states and all their arms and legs are working and they just choose not to work and instead to ask me for my hard earned money. It's time out for self-pity parties; those days are over. You've got to help yourself. Take a class when your child is in school. I know there are people who can't afford to go to school or take a class. But I have seen programs out there for parenting classes for free, and also trade school classes that are offered to low-income families. If you have a local library, use it and get some help.

Believe me, there are programs out there for a lot of things. But you have to be willing to help yourself and not wait until somebody knocks on your door with a bag of money and hands it to you.

Now back to the story. As I was saying, those Sunday bus rides inspired me in so many ways. I sometimes used to daydream about what I would do if I was rich or just well off. And growing up, the answers used to be, I was going to buy a big house and get a big fancy expensive car and look out for my family, and so on. As I got a little older I realized that sometimes helping people, including myself, is good; but it's better to show a person how to obtain certain things than just to give those things to them, because they might never know the hard work you put into something for them if they just take the handout. I'm not saying you shouldn't help people in need, but what some people need most is to help themselves, if you understand what I'm saying.

For me as a kid it was about clothes, cars, money and a big house. I'm not saying those items are bad, because there's nothing wrong with those things. It's just the concepts behind those things. I started asking myself as I grew up a little bit, if I had all those things, would I be happy and would my life be fulfilled, and would I live happily ever after? The truth was, no, because I realized things are just that—things. Things can't give you peace and love and joy that pass all understanding. I had to learn this the hard way, and here I'm just trying to make it a little easier for a person coming up to get a little food for thought.

Life is not about what you drive or how much money you earn on your job or how big your house is. Life is broken down into two parts: there are simple choices and decisions you make every morning you get out of bed, and these can be either good or bad. I myself have learned to make better choices—not because I'm perfect, by any means. But if I'm striving to be perfect, there's no room for poor choices and bad decisions. I find it very hard to believe, but you have some very smart and intelligent people who wake up in the morning and decide to make a choice and never think about the repercussion of that choice, whether it be good or bad. Now that I'm a little bit wiser I try my best to look at every angle before I take a frog leap off the cliff and try to blame somebody else for my bad choices.

Items like cars, houses, or money don't make you a man or a woman. It's integrity, honor, respect and dignity that will take you a long way in life. Those are just a few qualities which will get you on your way to a better, more successful life.

But try telling that to a seventeen-year-old boy, who thinks he is a full-grown man, living at home with his mama at 1057 West 14th street! I used to wonder sometimes, now I don't any more because I know: before you even enter into this world, God already has your life mapped out for you. He knows your beginning and your ending. Your destiny lies in his hands, and that includes your choices and decisions. Gods wants you to prosper and develop so you can be the very best that you can be, and have all the true riches and glory and eternal life in heaven.

Now I'm not trying to scare anybody away; I'm just trying to share with you how I got my bearings right. I'm not a preacher or anything, I'm just telling you the truth about my life and how this worked for me. And if it works for me, I know it will work for you. Again, it's your choice; you can try it and see for yourself.

I can make a choice to be sorry for myself and throw a pity party and wait for some man to lift me up, only to get let down because he can supply some of my needs but not all of my needs…. But I know someone who will supply and meet all my needs and it's greater than me and you, believe me.

I used to think if my father was here to see me grow up from a boy to a man and instill in me an image of what a man should be, I would have been better than I am today. That's a question I guess I will never find out the answer to. But I can make the decision to do the best that I can regardless of whether someone is watching or not. That's part of integrity right there, knowing what's right and doing what's right regardless of whether anyone is watching. I'm sure my father would have instilled that in me, or shown me that in some shape or form.

I think back to when I was in high school going to the Rainbow Library in Chicago on Roosevelt, watching people I went to school with and knowing how smart they are regardless of being poor, and learning how to ask for help and someone showing me where to get help. And over half the people I knew dropped out of school or had a child while still trying to attend school; or was on drugs or selling drugs, or in jail for a crime such as murder, and looking at the rest of his or her life behind bars. I go back and ask myself—I say, "Self, you could have taken many roads and made a left when you knew you should have made a right"—but someone was looking out for me and guided me in the right direction at the right time, at the right moment when I needed to be guided, and I thank him for that.

God puts people in your life for a certain reason, in a particular season, to develop your mind. It could be a family member or a friend, a teacher or preacher. I had all of the above, thank God, to show me right when I was wrong, and to show me wrong when I thought it was right—even though it took me a while to get it, and I'm still learning today. This day and age, you should be able to tell someone something positive and not get beaten over the head for your opinions. In this case some of these things I'm saying are opinions and some are facts but I will let you figure that out.

I myself have learned some things by trial and error, and I'm still learning. You are not simply a product of your environment, and your life is not destined for failure. Just because as a child you might have grown up poor, doesn't give you the right to rob somebody who is rich.

I'm just going to tell it the way I see it, so if you want to pull apart this book and find contradictions in it, be my guest. I wrote it for several reasons: to help others, to motivate others, to show others there are better ways of handling your life; and also to put my point of view across, to show that I'm living proof of a boy making bad choices becoming a man making good choices and better decisions. Believe me, it has not been easy, and I'm not going to sit here and sell you a peanut without the shell, and have you believe that a peanut doesn't have a shell on it. All I'm doing is cracking the shell open and letting you see for yourself what's in the inside.

Food for thought. Show yourself the way to improve; not depending on another man, because a man will let you down every time, but on yourself. Sit back and think, where did I make the wrong turn, and go back and redirect yourself and get on the right road. And don't put up roadblocks and say it's too late, I'm too old, and I don't have time to go back and change. These are just excuses, some of which I myself used until I realized that as long as I'm breathing in the morning, I can change and accept change in my life, and be delivered from the strongholds and struggles that I have had before. I can put these behind me and move forward.

Growing up I had to learn how to let go and say, "So what?" about what people may think or say about me. I just recently was delivered from a people-pleasing stronghold. You can't please everybody all the time. It's hard enough trying to please yourself, let alone everybody else—trying to make sure everyone around you is happy while you yourself are going crazy trying to make sure this is done and that is done so that people won't say anything bad about you. Even when you can't do it, you are borrowing, asking for help and whatever is needed so you won't look like you are letting that person or persons down. While in fact you yourself need help trying to maintain your own personal responsilties.

9

Kids Today

As my mother always told me, "People are going to talk about you regardless of what you do or don't do, so don't stress yourself. Help if you can and don't worry about it." And she was right. I can hand out a hundred dollars to two people: I can give one person a hundred dollar bill, and the other person I can give a hundred one dollar bills, and that person in this day and age would look at you and say why did you give me all these singles, while walking away counting the money you gave them. It's the same ungratefulness that a lot of kids today have, when they need to count their blessings.

I had some things but not a lot, and believe me, I was grateful for the few things I had. Today's children growing up want plasma screens, Play Station3's and X-box 360, and that's just in their playroom, not the bedroom…while the parent was raised in a bedroom the size of a closet, with just a bed and a set of headphones which you had to wait for, until your brother was done listening to them, or else you would fight all night about whether the batteries were going to run out.

Sorry about the sudden flashback. It's just amazing to me the lack of gratefulness kids have today. I talk to some kids today and they are talking on their cell phone at the age of nine years old. And I can't even recall having a house phone on a consistent basis until I was sixteen years old. I see kids that are not going to school unless they are wearing Phat Farm or f.u.b.u and a pair of latest Nike's. If that was me telling my mom that, I would have been wearing a blue body cast with a matching neck brace. Until you realize that you aren't paying the bills, while you are living under her roof you don't have a say in what you eating, wearing or any other thing you might decide you want. Today that sounds almost like prison.

The moral of this portion of the book is, be grateful for all that you have, and be appreciative if someone gives you something. Life is like a balancing scale; you are going to have good times and you are going to have bad times, but it's up to you how you are going to handle those times, regardless of what they are. Be strong and don't let any situation get the best of you. You're going to have times when it seems as if the storm and wind is never going to pass. But as we all know, storms can't last forever, only for a little while; and afterwards you can see the sun through the clouds shining so bright. It's the same with life's bad times: they too will pass and you will see brighter days ahead. It will make you strong and secure to know that if you made it through one storm you can make it through another.

10

The Great Depression

During the last year of high school I started to get very depressed and I just felt like I didn't care what people thought or how I felt about myself. I had a high school prom coming, but I used to just walk around the house in this deep depression. The first people to notice it was my friends I hung around with in the 'hood. They used to come by my house to get me and they'd say, "Dude tripping, he don't want to come out and kick it, and he's always clean-cut and his clothes are ironed and everything." Then the girl I was dating at the time and going to the prom with would come by and say, "You will be all right," and I would yell at her and slam the door in her face and treat her so bad. I apologized to her several times for that, after I got better.

My mom started to notice my behavior and immediately did what she thought was the best thing for me at the time, which was to take me to the doctor and get me checked out. The doctor told my mom that I had to take all these pills, and they made me even more depressed, so that I couldn't even move my arms or anything. Then she took me back to the doctor and they kept me this time, and ran some tests.

This is where it got crazy. If you are a person with a very weak mind, these people will have you believing you are crazy, when you are just depressed and in a funk phase. I watched these doctor give patients pills that didn't belong to them, mixing pills in their food, their ice cream; telling the patients they were trying out this new drug, and having parents to sign off on it, telling them it was for their own good. My mom didn't know that they were restraining people, taking needles and giving people shots to subdue them.

I recall this girl in the next room from me in the hospital; the security guard was raping her on the third shift when he came to work and no one believed her because they thought she was crazy or something. I used to go to school with this girl and I didn't think anything was wrong with her. She was smart, got good grades, and was attractive, but she took a lot of pills for her medical condition. I still see her from time to time in Circle Park Complex, and now she is doing much better. Her secret is safe with me. I will never expose her name, but I'm trying to reach out and help someone that might be going though this and feeling that they are the only one that went though a strange experience, and feeling too embarrassed to tell anyone about it.

During that time I had a lot of people coming to visit me at the hospital, and it helped a lot. I would like to take the time to thank those people for their support back then. I was later released from the hospital and was feeling a whole lot better because I stopped taking the pills and was flushing them down the toilet. And I started writing songs and poems and all that stupid stuff that was silly at the time, whatever got my mind free from what I had gone through. Don't be afraid to tell others about a problem you had, because you just might help someone who's going through a similar situation.

In the process of my situation I had hurt a girl who was my girlfriend at the time, and she had to miss the prom because of me and my great depression. My job was still there for me but I was so embarrassed that I didn't go back to it, and I found a new job. And I recall being upset with my mother because she didn't know what they did to those people in the hospital.

I have a few family members who have a similar problem with depression and they all handle it differently. I chose to act as if this never happened to me and that it was all a bad dream or something, but in reality it's been wearing me down not being able to talk to someone about it, except my baby sister. She'll understand where I'm coming from; she's a great listener. As time went on I started feeling better and I got myself back on the right track by self-motivation and perseverance, and not giving up hope for my dreams and future goals.

11

Stepping up to the Plate

I do believe that life at 1057 was like baseball. You never knew what the pitcher is going to throw you, whether it will be a curveball or fastball. If you stick with it, with practice and focus, sooner or later you're going to hit the ball. But it's up to the individual to keep their feet planted and keep an eye on the ball and connect with it, and at the right time you will hit one out the park. Every one has a home run in us; it just takes different things to bring it out of us.

I recall going to school and talking to my plumbing shop teacher about what I was going to do when I graduated from high school. I didn't have an answer. It was never really a big deal for me; I just thought I would do what I saw older men in the 'hood do. Which was work all day, and come home, have a beer and complain to their old ladies about the day. So then I started to think about what the teacher said to me and I went home and started looking into colleges. I even filled out a few applications, and got some responses, and I don't know what my excuse was for not going right away. The only thing I could think of was that I was afraid to leave the nest.

So I started going to school and talking to my shop teacher again and saying stuff like, my family doesn't have the money to pay for me to go to college. Of course he said that they have financial aid and other grant programs, which later in life became one of my best friends. He also explained to me how he went into the army and it helped him with money for school.

I went home and told my mother about the idea of college, and she of course supported me in whatever it was I wanted to do. But I knew she didn't have money for me to go to college. If I had wanted to go I should have been in school in the very beginning getting good grades so I could get a scholarship or something to help pay for it.

Moral of the moment: go to school with the intention to go to college, and do not take your education likely. Don't wait till the last couple of years of high school; and try to get serious about your life decisions.

Utilize your school counselors—that's what they get paid for, to help you with some of your decisions. I have made mistakes and I'm sure the person reading this book has made a few. But pick yourself up, look at what you're doing, acknowledge the area you need to change, and change it. Don't wait too long, because life does not promise that we have forever to make that change. But if you're breathing today, you can change.

I look at my mom as a mentor even though she didn't have a lot. She didn't give up and she stepped up to the plate swinging and hitting the ball when you really couldn't believe she had the strength to. That's when you think and say to yourself, I can do it, because I know someone that did make it though hard times and handled good times as well.

I believe that my mother knew right off the bat that her children had the potential to be and do whatever they put their minds to. But she also made it plain that you and only you have to get up and make it happen; and that no matter what a person says, if you can dream you can achieve. The sky is truly the limit. Don't let anybody tell you that you can't do something. You can do anything you put your mind to.

My mother never let you dwell on negativity too long, either. You can sit there and throw yourself a pity party while complaining, or you can do something about it. I learned that complaining doesn't solve the problem; if anything it adds to the problem. You have to make up your mind that you're going to come up with a solution to the problem and solve it. Otherwise you will end up playing the blame game, making excuses about why it's everybody else's fault that you're in the predicament that you're in. The blame game is when you blame everybody else about a situation that you got yourself into. I admit I used to play the blame game every time something didn't go the way I planned it. I had to blame someone or something; I couldn't just take the responsibility myself. I was going to go pro in the blame game; I was an M.V.P. (most valuable player) in the blame game back in the day.

12

Visiting Mil-Town

My brother moved to another state and I had just got to the point where I could understand a little better about relationships with your family and why it is important. I was still in school and he would come down and stay at 1057. I wanted to know so badly what life was like outside 1057. He would tell me how nice it was in Milwaukee, where he moved to. "Mil-town" is what they called it.

On my weekend off from school he would take me up there, and I was amazed at how far it was. It was like I was a slave or something, I would say to him as we drove all the way up north past Great America theme park and Gurnee, Illinois. I never knew this would be the first of many trips to and from Milwaukee.

Now I knew people existed in other states—wow, more girls. "Wait until I tell my guys," I thought. "We're going to make a few trips to Carl's mother's house."

I still wasn't sure what I was going to do. School was getting closer to ending and I didn't want to leave, so I spent more time procrastinating, not wanting to step up and make a decision on what I wanted to do in life.

Then my older sister Lesha left and moved to Milwaukee where my brother was living. This was not good for me because I used to go by her house and spend a night and get away from 1057 from time to time, like a mini-vacation or something. The reason she moved was to get out of the ghetto and away from the violent environment, with a gang shooting every other night. People were being killed right in the front of the row houses all through the village (that's what they called the housing project where she lived at the time). She just wanted a better life for her kids and she saw a way out, and rolled the dice and took a gamble on Mil-town.

My first impression of Milwaukee was weird, because I was used to seeing newer cars and guys would keep their hair cut and clean. I'm not saying Milwaukee was bad, just different. The guys rolled around in old-school cars with big tires, and had their hair done like Super Fly, and wore long nails.

I didn't see any trains or big high-rise project buildings. But they did have Park Lawn and West Lawn, low-income housing which were like the Chicago projects. What I did notice was that there was green grass in front of the houses, and no spray paint on the walls—whereas in the Chicago projects there was the famous urine smell in the hallways, and gang signs and R.I.P. spray paint all over the place—on buildings, cars, and even people's T-shirts. And of course grass in the projects in Chicago was just not going to happen. You had dirt paths, where people wore a groove in the path they would walk through on a daily basis.

Every building had is own identity, whether it was for which gang was the toughest, or whose building had the prettiest girls. Or who sold the best drugs, that were cheaper in price but good in quality. Now I drive by and some of the project buildings are being torn down and the tenants are being given low-income housing assistance so that they can build that area up again. The area is not far from downtown Chicago, and from the tenth floor you could see the skyline at night. On Lake Shore Drive that view will cost you a lot of money compared to low-income housing, where you pay next to nothing.

I know there are people that don't want to give up their housing for Section Eight (renter-assisted) housing. But people have bought that land and have plans for it, and those people that once lived there and made it their home now have to vacate and take whatever assisted housing they offer them. Some people may argue it's for the better, and some may argue it's for the worst. I myself have a mixed point of view on that whole situation.

13

Motherly Love

Back to 1057, my youngest sister Fatty had moved out into one of the project buildings. She didn't want to move but she was tired of my mother taking every penny she had when she got her check. Welcome to the club. My mother did that to everybody who had a job or income while living under that roof. Early in this book I told you she would give you the shirt off her back and give you money and everything.

I guess now it was time for her to reap what she sowed back then, by taking up her own collection plate every now and then. I didn't understand it at the time she was doing it, but in some strange way it helped instill in us a sense of character; that nothing in life is free, and that certain things cost money. When my baby sister Fatty moved back home she wasn't happy about it but understood somewhat what Mom's outlook was, and why she did what she did. I was glad Fatty was back because it meant that I didn't have to be there with the old lady by myself slaving away, doing all the house work.

Speaking of housework, now listen closely. My older brother Terry was still there but he was never at home, or he would always come home late. But he had a way with Mama when she might be mad at him; he had a system. He would come home and give her a kiss on the cheek first, and then put some money in her hand, and go upstairs, and then come downstairs later on and wash the dishes, before finally going upstairs to lay down. No questions asked, Mama would just smile and go to bed. I told you this guy had a way with women, including Mama.

Now I couldn't even think about doing this with Mama. First of all, when I come through the door she would be sitting at the kitchen table in her house coat waiting for the door to open. As soon as I opened the door she would swing a big log at my head, aiming for the side of my temple. Of course by now I have learned to duck, thanks to my other brother and sisters getting the life beat out of them in my early years. Then she would start to fuss at me, waving at my head with a mini axe hammer in her left hand. That is when you have a hammer on one side and an axe on the other. All the while she's screaming and hollering at me. Now mind you she's still got her right hand in her pocket waiting for me to say or do something stupid. That right pocket in her house coat is where she always keeps her .22 automatic, and the reason why she likes that gun is that when she shoots you, she said the .22 caliber bullet will travel slowly in your body. I know this woman was missing a few nuts and bolts.

Now you tell me why Terry got away with his system; I couldn't, and I'm the baby boy, the youngest of six. I was in fear of my life when the street lights came on. I was like Walter Payton of the Chicago bears trying to make it from wherever I was before the time of curfew.

My mother was nothing nice; she would hit you with whatever she got her hands on, and I am not lying. She would aim for your head all the time. I guess she figured if she hit you in the head, all your senses would get shaken up right. Now you please tell me where the hot line number is. Is there such a number at 1057? She would throw something at you quick, whether it was a can of corn or a dumbbell. One time—true story, I'm not making it up—she threw a bowling ball at my sister Neda's head, and lucky she ducked, because the wall had a bowling ball hole in their room when you come in the door. They later covered the hole in the wall with a poster of Prince from Purple Rain.

Not only would the old lady throw something at you, she would also swing at you with whatever she found lying around the house. Her favorite was a wooden log that she used to prop the dryer door so it would stay closed. This wooden log was huge; it was heavy too; but she used to carry it around like she was a pro wrestler, and intimated my friends if we were making too much noise in her house; and my friends would leave, so I guess it worked. My friends would say, "Man I am not going by your house, you liable to get shot or something."

My Mom would beat me with the handle of anything. She would hit me with a mop handle, broom handle, gun handle…no I'm just kidding about the gun handle, but all the rest are true. That old lady didn't show any fear, and she had no shame. She would beat you in front of your company or her company, out in public, in the grocery store…and nobody ever called a hotline number for me.

14

Parent's Nowadays

I respect, honor and thank my mom for every last whipping and punishment she ever put on me, and I never dreamed of raising my hand to hit her. This day and age parents believe that they have to be their kid's best friend and give them everything they want and ask for in order to be a good parent. My answer to that is a one-word answer: confused. These kids don't get any whipping, and I believe if you spare the rod you spoil the child. They don't appreciate their parents or listen to them. Nowadays these kids have too many choices, whereas when I was growing up you had one choice and one choice only, and that was the parents' choice.

Now don't get me wrong, I'm not parent-bashing. There are still a few who instill in their kids a sense of fear and let their kids know who the Mommy and Daddy is, and where the child's place is in the household. Also I'm not saying parenting is easy, because it's not. All I'm saying is this: if you're not capable or mature enough to raise a child, don't just have one anyway and let the streets raise him or her. Not to mention, don't let the prison system do the job of disciplining your children, when it was your job to begin with as a parent, and later play the blame game.

Moral moment: look deep before you make a life choice in bringing a life into this world without planning or preparing for his or her future. Also as parents make sure you both have common guidelines about how you want the child to be raised, from education to discipline. Not to leave out also, positive morals, values and beliefs that will some day help better equip your child. These are some tools that will help him or her later in life as a adult.

I see problems on a day-to-day basis, and to not say anything or do anything about them is the biggest problem that we as people have today. I'm not saying I as one person can save the whole world, but society and kids today need to know you're not alone. And there are people who want to see you succeed in life and not be another statistic. I know that inside every person they want to succeed in life, and that there will be several curveballs thrown at you, but you have to sometimes strike out or lose a game and then play the next game, so you have to watch what you did wrong in the first game in order to correct it and get it right and win. Giving yourself approval is one of life's keys—not for other people but for yourself. Knowing that you can achieve greatness if you just believe and be positive. If you have a goal or plan and stay focused it will happen.

As time went by I grew closer to completing high school. I still didn't have a clue about what I was going to do when I finished high school. This was sad because where I was from, getting a high school diploma was like getting a college degree, since so many people in the area I grew up in drop out of school.

I knew I had to do something and soon. Later my youngest sister moved to Milwaukee, and my mom and middle sister Neda and older brother Terry were still in Chicago at the time. Neda was living on the south side of Chicago, after moving out of the projects for some of the same reasons my sister Lesha did earlier—the shootings, killings, and the problems with drugs. That wasn't a good way to raise kids, let alone her little girls. If indeed you can do better than what you are capable of doing, then do it, which she did.

Time went on and later Neda moved to Milwaukee along with my youngest sister, and I was like, what the hell is going on. I had thought that one day we all would move to a warm place like Atlanta where it's nice and warm—not up north to Milwaukee. But I guess everything happens for a reason. My sister Lesha had asked me to move to Milwaukee after I finished high school, just until I was able to get on my feet and establish a goal or plan for what I was going to do in life.

So that gave me an option, which at the time I didn't have a lot of.

I knew I wanted to get out, and that could be a way out of 1057, so I could start something better and have a second chance to make a difference. So I told my sister, let me think about it. The first thing that came to mind was, I'm going to worry about Mama, and who's going to get on her last nerve, if I leave? I thought about it, and shortly after I finished high school I talked to a recruiter for the Marines, and he explained to me some options and plans. So I told him the same thing: give some time to think about.

I wish at the time, as a young man growing up, that I had a sense of what I wanted to be growing up, so I could reach out and achieve it, but I didn't. I had a counselor at the school, but I couldn't utilize that option now that I was out of school and clueless. Some people say timing is everything and being in the right place at the right time would make your life a whole lot better. I say God is everything, the beginning and the ending, so the right place and right time is where he wants you to be.

If you are in God's will and doing what's right, you know what's right all the time and accept Jesus Christ as your Lord and savior, and ask forgiveness of your sins, and have faith and believe; he will make it a whole lot better every time you turn around. Blessings will come down and curses will be lifted off your life.

Who knew, when I was a child at 1057, that I would have made the changes that I made, and adapted my lifestyle to that change, and would be committed to it. Life as I knew it had made a change, and 1057 was a part of that, and I can share a glimpse of what's yet to come in the new and upcoming book, *Adventures of Life in Milwaukee.* This a story about the choice I made once I decided to take my sister up on her offer to move to Milwaukee, and how I coped with the problems and struggles I had there, and what I did to overcome those struggles and problem. It's funny and serious and can help you understand a lot. Also it will give you a different outlook on things that might happen to you in your own life.

Special Thanks

At this time I like to thank God first and foremost for allowing me to Be Blessed to be a Blessing to others through putting a light on myself and sharing this book with others and not keeping it to myself.

I thank my wife and kids for putting up with me while adjusting and making changes. Also for supporting me in this decision to write a book based on true life experience and how I see it.

My mom whom I love, thank you for supporting me in everything. I promise I'm not going to worry about any negative feedback I get from this book.

To my brother's and sister's and the entire Sample family, I say thanks to all of you, and I hope you all receive a copy from me personally. God bless you all. Keep your head up and hold strong. Too my Nephews Ricky and little Monty. Son's Boogie and Sean and my Daughter Dee-Dee I hope you find something in this book you can use later in life but for right now keep those grades up. And you all well be in the next book because of how the story is being told love you all.

I dedicate this book to Richard L. Sample, Sr., God rest his soul, for giving me something to strive for and stand for. Hearing the kind of man he was has inspired me to do the right thing even when I see wrong. I thank God that man was my father.

978-0-595-37677-3
0-595-37677-0